C

Easy C Programming for Beginners

Your Step-By-Step Guide To Learning
C Programming

Felix Alvaro

Acknowledgments

Firstly, I want to thank God for giving me the knowledge and inspiration to put this informative book together. I also want to thank my parents, my brothers and my partner Silvia for their support.

Table Of Contents

Introduction

Congratulations on downloading the book *C: Easy C Programming for Beginners – Your Step-By-Step Guide to Learning C Programming*!

I understand that you're here, reading this copy of the book, because you want to know all about the C Programming language – what it is, what it does, how it can help you, and how to use the language to create programs.

Fear no more, as no other book can give you the answers but this one.

How can I be so sure? Well, the first part of the book contains the non-technical components of C programming: what it is, who was responsible for it, and where and when it started. You'll also learn what it can do and why you should learn this language.

The succeeding chapters will then deal with the technical details: codes, variables, loops, switch codes, if statements, and other related functions. Logic, identifiers, keywords and various types of operators will also be discussed, as well as command line arguments and other related topics.

You see, this book will be a great help to you – not only because you'll get to know the language that's used on most computers; this book will also help you create a program on your own using the C language. Plus, it'll be easier for you to branch out to other languages because C is a basic language that serves as a framework for the other programming languages. Want to learn C++, Java and other programming languages? Get to know C first.

I am honoured that with all the books you can find with the information you require, you chose to read mine. I can assure you, I have all the details you need, and I can be trusted with this topic. I can promise that with this book, you'll have everything you want to know and that you don't have to read any other book to satisfy your queries about the C programming language.

Time is ticking. Wait no more to learn about this language. Wasting your time not reading the book will mean days that you could have spent creating programs using C.

What are you waiting for? Start reading this book today!

In the first chapter, you will gain an understanding of C, its features, and the benefits of using such an amazing programming language.

Let's get to it!

Chapter One: The History of C Programming

In this chapter, you'll learn the basics – where C programming started, who created it, what C is all about, and why you should be using it.

Where It All Began

It was the '60s. Dennis Ritchie, along with other Bell Labs employees, was working on a project named Multics. He was aiming to create an operating system that can be used by a lot of people. Soon, Bell Labs had to withdraw from the project because they weren't able to come up with an economical and effective system, and so, Ken Thompson and Dennis Ritchie had to find another creation to work on.

Eventually, Thompson was able to develop a completely new system. It was first a version of the DEC PDP-7, but after a few tweaks and modifications, it became a system known as UNIX. UNIX also worked for the B programming language, which also was created by Ken Thompson. The problem with B was that it couldn't deal with data-types, as well as "structures", and so, Ritchie created the C programming language, which had all the functionality and power required to be used in an operating system.

What is C Programming?

C is a general high-level programming language ideal for creating various firmware or portable applications. C is one of the most used programming languages, as well as one of the oldest existing languages there is. It has led to the creation of other languages such as C++. It's one of the preferred languages because of its power and flexibility.

Even with its low-level proficiencies, C was made to promote cross-platform programming and has achieved a huge following, even in academic communities. It has also been standardized and made a part of POSIX, which stands for Portable Operating System Interface.

The first major creation using C was actually the Unix operating system. Because of that, Unix has been always connected to C. Today, however, C has become independent from Unix but is still viewed as an important language for every programmer to use.

It's good to learn C programming; it has been here for a while but because it's such a low-level language, but it's still very powerful and useful. It's a great way to get to learn other languages better. You'll find it easy to move om to other programming languages. C is also relatively easy to use for application development.

C Programming Features

What features does the C Programming Language offer? Here are some of them:

- It has this basic form of modularity; files can possibly be separately linked and compiled.

- You have a set number of keywords that includes control primitives i.e. if, for, switch, while and do while.

- Different assignments can be used in one statement.

- It offers different mathematical and logical operators with bit manipulators.

- You can choose to ignore function return values if not needed.

- Typing is static for C, but weakly enforced. All the data has type, yet can possibly be implicitly converted such as using characters as integers.

Benefits of C Programming

So why, with a lot of programming languages available right now, should you choose to study C?

It's because C still remains the priority language for a lot of reasons. C has remained a flexible and powerful language that you can use for varying programs – from engineering to business programs.

What is good about learning C?

- Since it has been around for 30 years, C has a lot of source codes available. This means you have a lot of room to learn about it, and you have a lot of methods to use.

- It's a small program, so you don't need an awful lot of memory to use it, compared to other languages. Don't belittle it, though; it's small but it's closer to assembly languages than other high-level ones, allowing you to create effective C codes.

- A lot of programmers are comfortable using C, and so it's almost close to being the mother tongue of programming.

- You can't learn Java or C++ directly unless you have a good grasp of programming elements. C, on the other hand, starts from scratch, which makes it easier to study compared to other programming languages.

- Programs such as Java, C++, and C# use Object Oriented Programming (OOP) and are still written using C.

- C can't be beaten in terms of performance, i.e. speed of executing programs.

- Drivers' devices are written in C because C gives you access to computers' basic elements. You can access your CPU memory through pointers, which help you manoeuvre your bits and bytes.

- Even PC games have C inside their cores, so that there can be faster responses to commands.

- Major components of operating systems, namely Linux, Unix and Windows, are still written using C language. This means you have to know C if you wish to program these systems; you'd even have the chance to create your own OS using C.

There is no other programming language that can be simpler, easier to use and more reliable than C. It gives you a lot of possibilities and a lot of opportunities to work on.

Want to work on a web app? C is a great language to start on. Want to create a game? C is also a reliable option. As previously mentioned, even an entire operating system can be written using C. C allows you to create useful and fun programs that everyone can enjoy.

In this chapter, you have learned about the basics and history of the C programming language, the most valuable features it offers as well as various benefits of using this language. In the next chapter, you will learn how to get started with C by installing the right software for you and your computer.

Chapter Two: How to Start Coding in C Language

In this chapter, I will guide you through the steps to get started with coding in C. Listen up!

One good thing about the C programming language is that you only need basic computer literacy. You don't need a specialization or skill to run it.

You'll need a C compiler to begin programming in C. **Compilers** are programs that convert C codes into running and executable machine codes.

Examples of compilers include Clang, Tiny C Compiler, GNU C Compiler, and Microsoft Visual Studio Express. All aforementioned programs run in Windows and some run using OS X or even Linux.

Minimum Software Requirements

To program in C, your computer must have a text editor, as opposed to having a word processor. Your plain text Notepad Editor may immediately come to mind. However, it won't be as effective because it lacks advanced capabilities such as debugging or code completion.

Recommended text editors include Sublime Text, Emacs, Vim, and Notepad++. These editors are equipped with line numbers and syntax highlighting – these features make your codes simpler and easier to read, plus you get to spot any syntax errors at a glance.

```
#include<stdio.h>

#include<stdio.h>   ●
1    #include<stdio.h>
2        int main()
3
4    {
5
6            printf("Hello World\n");
7
8            return 0;
9
10   }
```

Figure 1 Hello World Program on Sublime Text

There are programmers who choose to use an IDE or an Integrated Development Environment rather than to use a text editor. IDEs come with a bundle of programs that developers will use and benefit from, including a GUI or graphical user interface. These programs – text editor, project management, linker, and oftentimes a ready-to-use compiler and debugger – are grouped into a single convenient package.

Having IDEs may seem effective and convenient, but if you're a beginner who's just learning to code C, IDEs may not work for you because it hides the functions inside and you won't see what's going on. Going for the command line will make you more familiar with the process.

As a rule, go for the IDE if you know what the IDE does. If not, then don't use it and go for simpler methods instead.

Running Programs With C

C is what you call a compiled language. Writing programs in C means you have to use a compiler to read and run the data. The C program is the one that's human-readable, while the one that comes out of the compiler is the machine-readable one.

Your machine can only read the machine language – those streams of 0s and 1s, and so you need a compiler to convert human codes to machine ones.

Here are examples of compilers:

Name	Platform	License
Tiny CC Compiler (TCC)	Windows, GNU/Linux	LGPL
Clang	Windows, OS X, Unix, GNU/Linux	University of Illinois/NCSA License
Microsoft Visual Studio Express	Windows	Free Version
GNU C Compiler	MinGW(Windows), OS X, GNU/Linux	GPL

Let's say you chose to go for the GCC Compiler. Let me give you the instructions on how to download and install the program.

First Step: download and install Cygwin.

Cygwin will give you this Unix-like environment even when on a different OS like Windows. Download either the 32-bit or the 64-bit, depending on what your computer's version is.

Run the installer afterwards; the wizard will make you go through different steps. You'll soon arrive at this step, which is the 'Select Packages' step:

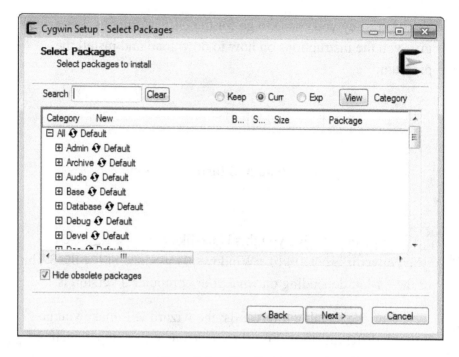

Figure 2: Installing Cygwin

Don't give yourself a headache in choosing just yet; just click 'Next' and proceed.

Soon, you'll be done with the installation, but don't delete your installers just yet; you'll need them in the future should you need to add or remove any parts of your packages.

Second Step: install the needed Cygwin packages.

You don't have to take note of a lot of packages; you can add them all in one go.

16

Open the Command Prompt, go to the folder where you have your Cygwin installer, and run this command:

```
C:\cygwin64>setup-x86_64.exe -q -P wget -P gcc-g++ -P make -P diffutils -P libmpfr-devel -P
libgmp-devel -P libmpc-devel
```

Once you've typed in this command, the system will automatically download all the necessary packages.

At this point, you've already succeeded in downloading and installing a working GCC compiler.

Third Step: building and installing the latest GCC.

Run a Cygwin terminal. To have the latest GCC source code, enter this command inside the Cygwin terminal:

```
$ wget http://ftpmirror.gnu.org/gcc/gcc-4.9.2/gcc-4.9.2.tar.gz
$ tar xf gcc-4.9.2.tar.gz
```

After entering this command, you should have a subdirectory named [gcc-4.9.2].

To configure the build, type this command afterwards:

```
$ mkdir build-gcc
$ cd build-gcc
$ ../gcc-4.9.2/configure --program-suffix=-4.9.2 --enable-
```

17

```
languages=c,c++ --disable-bootstrap --disable-shared
```

What do these commands mean?

- [--program-suffix=-4.9.2] – This means that upon GCC installation, it'll run as g++-4.9.2; it'll make it easier for the compiler to work with the system GCC compiler that Cygwin gave.
- [--enable-languages=c,c++] – This means only C and C++ compilers are installed in your system, and not those for Java, Go and Fortran.
- [--disable-bootstrap] – This means you'll be installing the compiler once; default installation will make the system install the compiler thrice for performance and quality issues.
- [--disable-shared] – This means the compiler built isn't installed as a DLL shared with other C++ applications.

Fourth Step: trying out the new compiler!

Let's test the compiler out by compiling codes using generic lambdas.

Create a file with a filename of [test.cpp] with these contents:

18

```
#include <iostream>

int main()
{
    auto lambda = [](auto x){ return x; };
    std::cout << lambda("Hello generic lambda!\n");
    return 0;
}
```

Now let's try compiling it using Cygwin's system GCC compiler:

```
$ g++ --version
$ g++ -std=c++1y test.cpp
```

If the version in your system isn't 4.9, then you'll get an error:

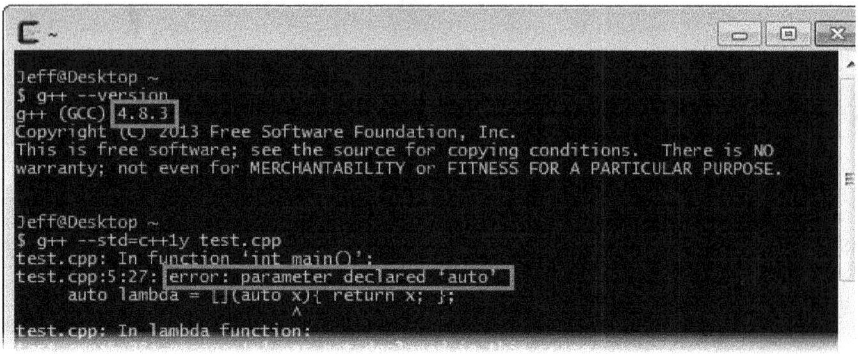

Figure 3: Cygwin error

But since you've got your own GCC compiler, you can just run it instead:

```
$ g++-4.9.2 -std=c++14 test.cpp
$ ./a.exe
```

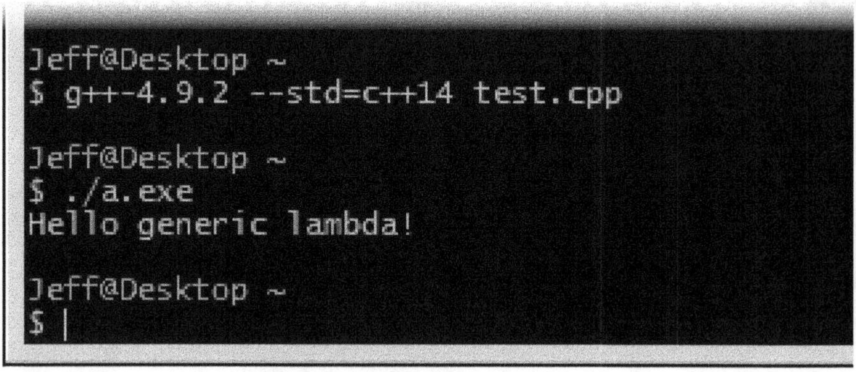

Figure 4: Running Your Program

20

If you follow all the steps correctly, then you'll see it work!

Alternatively, you can go the online compiler route. Visit the page below and run your codes from there:

https://www.codechef.com/ide

Let's paste the same Hello World program and see the results:

Figure 5: Using codechef.com

Click on the Run button at the bottom to execute the code. If your code needs a user input, tick the Custom Input box. The output will be shown at the bottom section.

Figure 6: Output

We will be using Code Chef for all examples in this book.

In this chapter, I have shown you how to get up and running with the right software, so that you can begin running programs with C. The upcoming chapter is one of the most crucial chapters, as I will be showing you how to structure your codes correctly. I will discuss Variables, If Statements, Loops and much more.

Chapter Three: Getting to Know Program Variables

In this chapter, you will learn how to start defining variables for your program.

When it comes to C Programming, you need to make use of a certain structure that contains a group of related values. This way, the program gets to be more modular—it becomes easier to understand.

When values are grouped together, you can form a certain program that has some uniformity. For example, a game or a contact list. For this, you have to use the following syntax:

```
struct Tag {

all parts of the struct in this area

};
```

In order to structure codes, you also have to keep in mind that there are certain functions that you have to use such as variables.

Variables

Variables help you easily declare parameters for your program. Remember these syntax rules governing variable names:

- Allowed characters: capital letters, small letters, numbers (0-9), and underscore
- Not allowed: Blank spaces, commas, and symbols other than the underscore
- Not allowed: Using reserved words (such as *int*, *char*, *continue*) as variable names
- The first character of the variable name should be an underscore or a letter
- Variable names are case-sensitive.

Here are a few examples of what are considered valid and invalid variable names:

Var_name2 – The variable contains underscores, numbers, and letters, which are all VALID characters.

2var_name - Starts with a number therefore is INVALID.

Var_name%- Contains the percentage (%) sign. INVALID.

.2var_name - Starts with a dot. INVALID.

_var_name - This starts with an underscore (_) and is considered VALID.

CONTINUE – The reserved word is *continue,* and since C is case-sensitive, this is a VALID variable name. However, to avoid confusion, we recommend not using any reserved words regardless of the letter case.

Variable Data Types

There are three different forms of variables:

- Numeric Integer: pertaining to whole numbers
- Numeric Real: used for numbers with floating points and decimal places
- Character: ASCII characters and numbers can be used as long as these are declared within single quotes (eg. 'First 123 code')

Type-name	Type	Range
int	Numeric – Integer	-32 768 to 32 767
short	Numeric – Integer	-32 768 to 32 767
long	Numeric – Integer	-2 147 483 648 to 2 147 483 647
float	Numeric – Real	1.2×10^{-38} to 3.4×10^{38}
double	Numeric – Real	2.2×10^{-308} to 1.8×10^{308}
char	Character	All ASCII characters

Figure 7: Different Type-names

25

Declaring Variables

In C, declaring a variable simply involves putting the type-name and the variable name.

Here's how it is done:

```
int main()
{
        int ThisIsAnIntegerVariable;
        char ThisIsACharacterVariable;
        return 0;
}
```

You can also declare multiple variables at the same time.

```
int main()
{
        int var1, var2, var3;
        return 0;
}
```

If you wish to immediately initialize or assign a value to a parameter, you can do this by using the syntax below:

```
int main()
{
        int var1=1;
        char name= 'Linda';
        return 0;
}
```

To demonstrate how variable declaration and initialization works, here's an exercise using a simple code:

```c
#include <stdio.h>

// Variable declaration:
extern int A, B;
extern int C;
extern float D;

int main () {

    /* variable definition: */
    int A, B;
    int C;
    float D;

    /* actual initialization */
    A = 10;
    B = 20;

    C = A + B;
    printf("What is C? : %d \n", C);

    D = 20.0/6.0;
    printf("What is D? : %f \n", D);

    return 0;
}
```

The result of the program is this:

```
What is C? : 30
What is D? : 3.33333
```

Did you get it right?

Reserved words

Next up are keywords. These are the reserved words that are used in C Programming, which also includes identifiers and some special characters.

The main keywords used are the following:

auto	double	int	struct
break	else	long	switch
case	enum	register	typedef
char	extern	return	union
const	float	short	unsigned
continue	for	signed	void
default	goto	sizeof	volatile
do	if	static	while

Figure 8: Reserved words in C

I will briefly discuss the reserved words that are not discussed in this book. All the rest are covered in the chapters of this book.

Enum. As the name suggests, this is used to enumerate certain parts of the program. This consists of constant integers. For example:

```
enum enum_var{
    var4;
    var5;
    var6;
};
```

Short, long, unsigned. These are **Auto**. This is used to define storage class variables. For example:

auto int var1;

Const. This means constant, which means that there is a constant value in the program. For example:

const int a=10;

Double and Float. This is used to indicate float type variables and used for respective data. For example:

Float thisvariable

Double thisvariable

Extern. This denotes that external variables are around and is accessed and declared through different functions. For example:

mostly used for integers, and for this, you have to take note of the following ranges:

Short int (-32768 to 32767)

Unsigned int (0 to 655355)

Signed int (-32768 to 32767)

Long int (-32768 to 32767)

Return. This terminates the current function's execution and gives some value back to the function itself. For example:

```
int func(){

int b=10;

return c;

}
```

Static. This is used to indicate the storage class' value and could be used until you reach the end of the program. For example:

```
Static int var;
```

Register. This is something that differentiates normal variables from fast ones. For example:

```
Register int var1;
```

Typedef. This helps you differentiate simple numbers from integers. For example:

```
Typedef float ab;

Ab butterfly, wings
```

Struct. This is used to create structures so they could easily be managed. For example:

```
struct contestant{

char name[1116];
```

30

```
float marks;

int age;

}s2,s3;
```

Void. This means that a part of your program has no value. For example:

```
void no_return(int a){

.....

}
```

Union. Union is about handling the variables. This is what you have to do:

```
union student {

char name[100];

float marks;

int age;

}
```

Volatile. This means that you have an erroneous function in your program. This is what you have to do:

```
const volatile number
```

There are also special characters that you can use, and these are:

$, \diamond . \_ () ; \$: \% [] \# ? \text{ ' } \& \{\} \text{ " } \wedge ! * /|\text{-}\backslash\sim+$

As for digits, you can use the following:

0 1 2 3 4 5 6 7 8 9

You can also use uppercase or lowercase alphabet letters, as well.

Creating Constants

C language allows you to create constants – a parameter whose value cannot be changed in the program.

Here's the syntax:

```
cons int multiplier=100
```

In this code, we'll create a constant and attempt to change its value within the program:

```
#include<stdio.h>

int main()

{

   const int multiplier = 100;
   int a = 10;
   int b = 3;
   int c;
   int d;
```

32

```
        c = a + b;
        printf ("c is the sum of a and b. The
value of c is %d\n", c);

        multiplier = 1;
        d = multiplier * c;

        printf ("d is the product of
multiplier and c. The value of d is %d\n", d);

        return 0;


    }
```

Did you get the same error as below?

Compile Info

```
prog.cpp: In function 'int main()':
prog.cpp:16:14: error: assignment of read-only variable 'multiplier'
    multiplier = 1;
              ^
```

Once you create a constant, you can use the parameter inside the program anytime you need it. In the next example, we will use the parameter to multiply and add within the code.

```c
#include<stdio.h>

int main()

{

    const int multiplier = 100;
    int a = 10;
    int b = 3;
    int c;
    int d;

    c = a + b;
    printf ("c is the sum of a and b. The
value of c is %d\n", c);

    d = multiplier * c;

    printf ("d is the product of
multiplier and c. The value of d is %d\n", d);

    c = multiplier + a;
    printf ("c is the sum of multiplier
and a. The new value of c is %d\n", c);

    return 0;


}
```

Here is the output:

```
c is the sum of a and b. The value of c is 13
d is the product of multiplier and c. The value of d is 1300
c is the sum of multiplier and a. The new value of c is 110
```

Figure 9: Creating Constants

Line Breaks

You may have noticed that we frequently use \n in our code to signify a new line. Aside from \n, here are other escape characters that you can use:

Escape Sequences

Escape Sequences	Character
\b	Backspace
\f	Form feed
\n	Newline
\r	Return
\t	Horizontal tab
\v	Vertical tab
\\	Backslash
\'	Single quotation mark
\"	Double quotation mark
\?	Question mark
\0	Null character

Figure 10: Escape Characters

Now that you already know how to declare and initialize a parameter or variable in your program, let's take a look at how you can introduce complex actions to your program using operators. We'll have more of these in the next chapter.

Chapter Four: Operators

In this chapter, you will understand how you can make your program achieve complex tasks—all with the help of Operators! Conditions and operations are the heart of every programming language. These are the things that make your program capable of computing and evaluating inputs and variables.

Operators

There are several types of operators that you can use in C:

1. Assignment Operators
2. Arithmetic Operator
3. Relational Operators
4. Logical Operators
5. Miscellaneous Operators

Assignment Operators

Assignment Operators are used to assign variables their values. Here are some of the basic assignment operators:

Operator	Description
=	Basic assignment. Use this to assign any value to a variable. A= B + C
+=	Add and assign value. A += B translates to A = A + B
-=	Subtract and assign value. A —= translates to A = A - B
*=	Multiply and assign value A *= B translates to A = A * B
/=	Divide and assign value A /= B translates to A = A / B
%=	Get modulus and assign value A %=B translates to A = A % B

Use the codes below to demonstrate how these operators are used:

```c
#include<stdio.h>

int main()

{

    int a = 3;
    int b = 9;
    int c ;

    c = a + b;
        printf ("c is the sum of a and b. The
value of c is %d\n", c);
```

```
        c+=a;
        printf ("c is the sum of c and a. The
new value of c is %d\n", c);

        c-=a;
        printf ("c is the difference of c and
a. The new value of c is %d\n", c);

        c*=b;
        printf ("c is the product of c and b.
The new value of c is %d\n", c);

        c/=a;
        printf ("c is the quotient of c and a.
The new value of c is %d\n", c);

        return 0;


    }
```

Here's the output:

Output

```
c is the sum of a and b. The value of c is 12
c is the sum of c and a. The new value of c is 15
c is the difference of c and a. The new value of c is 12
c is the product of c and b. The new value of c is 108
c is the quotient of c and a. The new value of c is 36
```

Figure 11: Assignment Operators Exercise

Arithmetic Operators

Arithmetic Operators allow you to perform formulas with variables. Here are some of the basic arithmetic operators. Let's use the values: a = 3 and b = 9.

Operator	Description
+	Add the values a + b = 12
-	Perform subtraction b – a = 6
*	Perform multiplication a*b = 27
/	Perform division b/a = 3
%	Modulus – show the remainder after division b/a = 0
++	Add one a++=4
--	Subtract one b--=8

Let's put these into action:

```
#include<stdio.h>

int main()

{

    int a = 3;
    int b = 9;
    int c ;

    c = a + b;
    printf ("c is the sum of a and b. The
value of c is %d\n", c);

    c = b - a;
```

41

```c
        printf ("c is the difference of b and
a. The new value of c is %d\n", c);

        c = a * b;
        printf ("c is the product of a and b.
The new value of c is %d\n", c);

        c = b/a;
        printf ("c is the quotient of b and a.
The new value of c is %d\n", c);

        c = b%a;
        printf ("c is the modules of b and a.
The new value of c is %d\n", c);

        a++;
        printf ("a is the value of a + 1. The
new value of a is %d\n", a);

        b--;
        printf ("b is the value of b - 1. The
new value of b is %d\n", b);

        return 0;

}
```

Paste the code above on CodeChef and see if you get the same results as below:

Output

```
c is the sum of a and b. The value of c is 12
c is the difference of b and a. The new value of c is 6
c is the product of a and b. The new value of c is 27
c is the quotient of b and a. The new value of c is 3
c is the modules of b and a. The new value of c is 0
a is the value of a + 1. The new value of a is 4
b is the value of b - 1. The new value of b is 8
```

Figure 12: Arithmetic Operators Exercise

Relational Operators

Relational Operators are used to compare variables, and return a Boolean result of the evaluation. This means it will signal the program if the value is True or False. Let's use the same values: a = 3 and b = 9.

Operator	Description
==	Check for equality a == b; FALSE
!=	Check for inequality a =! b; TRUE
>	Greater than
<	Less than
>=	Greater than or equal to a >= 3; TRUE
<=	Less than or equal to a <= 3; TRUE

To see how this works, we will use the *if* statement which will be discussed further in Chapter 5. For now, copy and paste the code below on CodeChef.

```
#include<stdio.h>

int main()

{

    int a = 3;
    int b = 9;

    if (a==b) {
    printf ("Values a and b are equal \n");
    }
    if (a!=b) {
    printf ("Values a and b are not equal
\n");
```

43

```
        }
        if (a>b) {
        printf ("a is greater than b \n");
        }
        if (a<b) {
        printf ("b is greater than a \n");
        }
        if (a>=3) {
        printf ("a is greater than or equal to
3 \n");
        }
        if (a<=3) {
        printf ("a is less than or equal to 3
\n");
        }

        return 0;


    }
```

Did you get the same output messages?

Output

```
Values a and b are not equal
b is greater than a
a is greater than or equal to 3
a is less than or equal to 3
```

Figure 13: Relational Operator Exercise

Logical Operators

Next, let's get to logical operators. These operators test and compare the output of a statement or condition. The test will either return a True or False value. Let's use the same values: a = 3 and b = 9 and add these values: c = 2, d = a - 1

Operator	Description
||	OR operator . The condition becomes true when the logical state of any of the operands is true. ((a ==b) || (c ==d)) evaluates to TRUE
&&	AND operator. This returns true when all of the operands evaluate to true. ((a ==b) && (c ==d)) evaluates to FALSE
!	NOT operator. It's used to reverse the result of the condition. If the condition below evaluates it to True, using the NOT operator will reverse it to False. !((a ==b) && (c ==d)) evaluates to TRUE

Logical operators make way for assignment, arithmetic, and relational operators to come together in a condition. The logical operator will be used to evaluate the condition. Here's a short code to showcase how logical operators work.

```c
#include<stdio.h>

int main()

{

    int a = 3;
    int b = 9;
    int c = 2;
    int d = a - 1;

    if ((a==b) || (c ==d))   {
    printf ("OR Operator: Print this when
one or both of the conditions is true \n");
    }
    if ((a ==b) && (c ==d)) {
    printf ("AND operator: Print this when
both of the conditions are true\n");
    }
    if (!((a ==b) && (c ==d))) {
    printf ("NOT operator: Print this when
the condition becomes true");
    }
    return 0;


}
```

Here's the output that you should get once you run this on
CodeChef:

Output

```
OR Operator: Print this when one or both of the conditions is true
NOT operator: Print this when the condition becomes true
```

Figure 14: Logical Operators Exercise

47

To validate the output, change the values of the inputs and run the code again. Come up with values that will output the message for the AND operator.

Miscellaneous Operators

The C language also gives us other useful operators:

Operator	Description
sizeof	Checks for the variable size – reflects the size of storage for the variable type
? :	Ternary operator: outputs value a if condition is true, otherwise b will be shown

Here's a short code to show how ternary operators and sizeof work:

```
#include <stdio.h>

int main() {

    int first = 4;
    char second='x';
    int a;
    int b;

    printf("This is the size of the first
variable = %d\n", sizeof(first) );
    printf("This is the size of the second
variable = %d\n", sizeof(second) );

    a = 3;
    b = (a == 3) ? 100: 200;
    printf( "Therefore, the value of b is
%d\n", b );
```

```
        b = (a == 11) ? 200: 300;
          printf( "Therefore, the value of b is
%d\n", b );
    }
```

Add other variable types to see what is the storage size:

Output

```
This is the size of the first variable = 4
This is the size of the second variable = 1
Therefore, the value of b is 100
Therefore, the value of b is 300
```

Figure 15: Miscellaneous Operators Output

Values

Values basically pass arguments to the various copies in your function, where you have to make changes in the parameters. For this, the *swap()* function is necessary. For example:

```c
#include <myfavoriteprogram>

/* Declare this function */

void swap(int x, int y);


int main () {

  /* local variable definition */

  int a = 200;

  int b = 400;

  printf("Value of a before swap: %d\n", a );

  printf("Value of b before swap : %d\n", b );


  /* Swap the values with the use of a function */

  swap(a, b);


  printf("Value of a after swap : %d\n", a );

  printf("Value of b after swap : %d\n", b );


  return 0;
```

In this chapter, we covered Logic, Keywords and Operators. In the next chapter, you will learn all that you need to know about loops and loop break statements.

Chapter Five: Decisions, Loops, and Functions

Decision Statements

If Statements

If Statements give you the ability to control your program's flow, so that it will be easier for you to manage. If statements are governed by test conditions, and if any of these conditions evaluate to true, the specific action will be applied. These statements are also used for cover user-defined passwords, CAPTCHA codes, and anything else that could add security.

The basic If syntax is:

if (statement is TRUE)

Execute this line of code

So, for example:

if (10 + 10 = 20)

printf("20 is the sum of two tens");

As you can see, if the condition 10+10 is satisfied, the phrase "20 is the sum of two tens" will be shown on the screen.

But what happens when the condition is false? This is where Else statements come in. Else provides the action to be performed if the condition turns out to be false. In the case of nested ifs, Else is a catchall in case nothing evaluates to true. For example, if someone inputs the wrong email or password, then you'd see things like *"Forgotten Password?"* or *"Not the right email address"* onscreen. That's how Else Statements work.

Use any of the applicable operator to test for the condition in your if statements. Take note of the comments starting with /* to know what the line of the code does.

Here's a good example of a nested-if code:

```c
#include <stdio.h>

int main()
{
    int age;
        printf( "Please enter your age:\n" );
        scanf( "%d", &age );
        if ( age<18) {
            printf ("You are not allowed" );
        }
        else if ( age == 18 ) {
            printf( "You are old enough\n" );
        }
        else {
            printf( "You are allowed\n" );
        }
    return 0;
}
```

Enter a value of 4 in the custom input field and see the result:

Figure 16: If Statement

Change the input value to validate the output of the code.

Switch Cases

Meanwhile, if you have several specific conditions to test, you can make use of switch cases—also known as switch statements. There are certain rules that you have to follow, though, and these are:

1. Switch statements could also be default cases. Therefore, they have to appear at the end of the switch and could be

54

used to determine false statements in the program. In this case, you wouldn't have to use a break anymore.

2. You don't need a break for every case. In case no break appears, all you have to do is wait for something to fall through.

3. When you have reached the break statement, go ahead and change the terminates that you have been using so that you could then jump to the next line.

4. Constant Expression should be used. This means you have to use the same data types in your program.

5. Every switch contains a number of case statements that could be separated with colons.

6. You could use enumerated or integral types of switches so that class conversion could easily be done.

For this, you have to remember that:

Expression → Case 1 → Code Block 1

→ Case 2 → Code Block 2
→ Case 3 → Code Block 3

Use the following simple code to see how case statements work. Take note of the *break* command as this will be discussed in the Decision Break section.

```
#include<stdio.h>
 int main()
 {
        char userinput;
```

```c
        printf("which subject is your
favorite?\n");
        printf("A: Math\n");
        printf("B: Science\n");
        scanf("%c", &userinput);

        switch (userinput)
        {
            case 'A':
                printf("welcome
to your Math class!\n");
                break;
            case 'B':
            {
                printf("Let's go
learn about Science!\n");
                break;
            }
            default:
                printf("Subject
does not exist\n");
                break;
        }
        return 0;
    }
```

Entering either A or B will result to any of the statements being printed on the screen. If, for example, you did not enter any of the options correctly, the program will display the default message. Remember that C is case-sensitive, so entering *a* will result to the program showing the default message.

Input

```
a
```

Output

```
Which subject is your favorite?
A: Math
B: Science
Subject does not exist
```

Figure 17: Case Statement

Loops

Most of the time, programs require running the same algorithm several times. Loops can be used to make repetitive algorithms easier to code.

There are four types of loops:

- for loop
- while loop
- do while loop

Each loop differs in functionalities, so you'll have to study and practice working with each one to know which one you should use for your code.

For Loop

In case you need to print "I know how to code!" ten times, how would you do it?

You can opt to do ten lines of printf on your code but what if the number of times is a user-input? This is where for loops can help.

For loops repeat an action for x number of times.

Syntax:

> for (beginning value; condition that should be true to continue; statement for value increment)

Here's a sample code:

```
#include<stdio.h>
int main()
{
                int printtimes, counter;
```

```
                printf( "How many times do
you want to print this?\n" );
                scanf( "%d", &printtimes );
                for (counter = 0; counter <
printtimes; counter++)
                {
                        printf ("I know how to
code!\n");
                }
            return 0;
    }
```

Enter the number of times that you would like to print the phrase:

Input

```
5
```

Output

```
How many times do you want to print this?
I know how to code!
I know how to code!
I know how to code!
I know how to code!
I know how to code!
```

Figure 18: For example

While Loop

The while loop is used when conditions must be satisfied for the while condition to run.

Syntax:

> while (condition is true, do the following lines)

Let's take the same example above to display how while works. Before printing the line, let's check if it will exceed the screen length.

```
#include<stdio.h>
int main()
{
            int    printtimes,    sclength,
counter;
            sclength = 4;
            printf( "How  many  times  do
you want to print this?\n" );
            scanf( "%d", &printtimes );
            counter=0;
            while          ((counter      <
printtimes) && (printtimes < sclength))
            {
                  counter++;
                  printf ("I know how to
code!\n");
            }
         return 0;
    }
```

Next, input a value less than the screen length. You should get the same output below:

Input

```
3
```

Output

```
How many times do you want to print this?
I know how to code!
I know how to code!
I know how to code!
```

Figure 19: While example

Now, put an input greater than the value of the screen length and see what you get.

Do…While Loop

The do while loop is similar to the while statement, except that it performs an action first before checking for the condition.

Syntax:

```
do
{ action;
}
while (condition is true);
```

We'll tweak the while loop code and convert it to a do-while loop.

```c
#include<stdio.h>
int main()
{
    int printtimes, sclength, counter;
    sclength = 4;
    printf( "How many times do you want to print this?\n" );
    scanf( "%d", &printtimes );
    counter=0;
    do
    {
        counter++;
        printf ("I know how to code!\n");
    }
    while ((counter < printtimes) && (printtimes < sclength));
    return 0;
}
```

Now, if you use the number 3 as your input for *printtimes*, you'll get a similar output as when using the while loop.

Try to use the number 4 now, or any value greater than *sclength*. Did you get the same result?

Input

```
5
```

Output

```
How many times do you want to print this?
I know how to code!
```

Figure 20: Do-while example

Because the do-while statement performs an action first, before checking the condition, one line will be printed, even when the *printtimes* is greater than *sclength*.

Use the same input with the while statement and see the difference between the two loop statements.

Decision Break Statements

Goto Statement

During the course of a loop statement, you may want to exit the loop during certain conditions. One option that you can use is the goto statement.

The goto statement exits a loop when a condition is satisfied, and goes back to the specified statement.

Here's our scenario: Let's count to ten but let's skip all multiples of 3. Use the code below to implement this.

```c
#include <stdio.h>

int main () {
    int value;
    value=0;
    THREES:do {
        if((value % 3) == 0) {
        value++;
        goto THREES;
    }
    printf("Watch me count without multiples
of 3: %d\n", value);
    value++;
    }while( value < 10 );
    return 0;
}
```

As expected, the output should skip numbers 3, 6, and 9.

Output

```
Watch me count without multiples of 3: 1
Watch me count without multiples of 3: 2
Watch me count without multiples of 3: 4
Watch me count without multiples of 3: 5
Watch me count without multiples of 3: 7
Watch me count without multiples of 3: 8
Watch me count without multiples of 3: 10
```

Figure 21: Go-To statement

Continue Statement

This statement simply means that the program should skip the rest of the loop statements and start from the beginning of the loop again.

Use this simple code to demonstrate how continue statements work.

```c
#include<stdio.h>

int main()
{
        int counter;
counter = 0;
                while ( counter < 5 )
                {
                        counter++;

    printf("%d\n",counter);
                        continue;
                        printf("will  you
see this line printed?\n");
                }
                return 0;
        }
```

65

In the output, you'll notice that the line was never printed because of the preceding continue statement.

Figure 22: Continue Statement

Break Statement

To terminate a loop, you can use the break statement. Once the condition is met, the program will exit the loop.

In this example, once the variable *ct* becomes greater than 5, the program will exit the loop.

```
#include <stdio.h>

int main () {
    int ct = 1;
```

```c
/* while loop execution */
while( ct < 8 ) {

    printf("Current ct value is: %d\n", ct);

    ct++;

    if(ct > 5) {
        break;
    }

}
printf ("Out of the loop!");
    return 0;
}
```

Here is how the output should turn out:

Output

```
Current ct value is: 1
Current ct value is: 2
Current ct value is: 3
Current ct value is: 4
Current ct value is: 5
Out of the loop!
```

Figure 23: Break Statement

Functions

Functions are chunks of code that needs to be performed a number of times. To organize and manage programs efficiently, you can put a specific task inside a function. Once the program needs to perform the function, you can simply call the function within the code.

Here's a quick demonstration of how a function works:

Run this code on CodeChef.

```
#include<stdio.h>
void FunctionTest()
{
        printf("This line is from
FunctionTest.\n");
}
int main()
{
        FunctionTest();
        return 0;
}
```

Did you see the `This line is from FunctionTest` output?

Next, let's try using a function in a way that is applicable to your program. Suppose you are to create a function that adds any two numbers and can be called anytime within the program.

68

```c
#include<stdio.h>

int AddNumbers(int output1,int output2 )
{
        printf("%d\n", output1);
        printf("%d\n", output2);
        return output1 + output2;
}

int main()
{
        int answer1, input1, input2;

        scanf("%d\n", &input1);
        scanf("%d", &input2);

        answer1 =
AddNumbers(input1,input2);

        printf(" The sum of these numbers
is %d\n", answer1);

        int multiply, answer2;
        answer2 =
((AddNumbers(input1,input2))*2);
        printf(" The sum of these numbers
multiplied by 2 is %d\n", answer2);
        return 0;
}
```

Now, enter 2 integers as your input.

Input

```
1
3
```

Output

```
1
3
 The sum of these numbers is 4
1
3
 The sum of these numbers multiplied by 2 is 8
```

Figure 24: Output of a Function

In this chapter, you have learned how to create different loop and loop break statements. You've also demonstrated how functions work in a program. In the next chapter, I will discuss arrays and pointers.

Chapter Six: Pointers, Arrays, and Strings

To make your code more efficient, you need to make use of pointers, arrays, and strings—and you'll learn about them in this chapter! They may sound complicated, but they're actually quite easy to learn!

Arrays

Arrays provide the functionality of declaring all possible values inside one variable. For example, you want to declare all the months for your quarterly payment. Instead of assigning a variable for months 3, 6, 9, and 12, you can simply create an array for *month*.

```
int month[4];
```

Next, assign values to the array.

```
int month[4];
month[0] = 3;
month[1] = 6;
month[2] = 9;
month[3] = 12;
```

To print a value from the array, use the line below:

```
printf("%d",month[3]);
```

Structures

A structure is something that is used to represent a record. Structures is also known as *Struct Statement*. For example, for a book, you have the title, the author, or the number of pages. For food, you have ingredients, instructions on how it was made, and who made it. For example:

```
struct Recipe Book {

char  title[50];

char  author[50];

char  topics[100];

int  book_id;

} book;
```

/* book 1 specification */

```
strcpy( Book1.title, "Sheperd's Pie");

strcpy( Book1.author, "Gordon Ramsay");

strcpy( Book1.subject, "Recipe Books");

Book1.book_id = 6495407;
```

/* book 2 specification */

```
strcpy( Book2.title, "Cooking Like a Masterchef");

strcpy( Book2.author, "Graham Elliot");

strcpy( Book2.subject, "Recipe Books");

Book2.book_id = 6495700;
```

Pointers

Pointers are variables that take on the address of another variable. They're like memory locators. For this, you have the following:

```
char  *ch    /* pointer to a character */

double *dp;  /* pointer to a double */

float *fp;   /* pointer to a float */

int   *ip;   /* pointer to an integer */
```

Here's a good example:

```c
#include <myfavoriteprogram>


int main () {


    int var = 18;   /* declaration of variable */
    int *ip;        /* pointer variable declaration */


    ip = &var;  /* var storage address here*/


    printf("Address of var variable: %x\n", &var );


    /* The address is in the pointer variable */
    printf("Address stored in ip variable: %x\n", ip );


    /* access the value using the pointer */
    printf("Value of *ip variable: %d\n", *ip );


    return 0;

}
```

Strings

There are also Strings in C Programming. Strings are mostly used to resemble quotes, or to add quotes into your program. Remember that strings are simply a collection or array of articles terminated by a null or \0 character.

For this, you have to remember the following:

1. You can insert double quotes in a string by beginning and ending with a single quote.

2. Single or double quotes could both be used at the beginning of the string.

3. You can't insert double quotes on a string that begins and ends with double quotes.

4. You can insert single quotes in a string that begins with double quotes.

5. You can't insert single quotes in a string that begins and ends with single quotes.

Here's a sample of a code using a string as an array:

```c
#include<stdio.h>

int main()
{
        char teststring[20];

        teststring[0] = 'T';
        teststring[1] = 'E';
        teststring[2] = 'S';
        teststring[3] = 'T';
        teststring[4] = '\n';
        teststring[5] = '\0';

        printf("%s", teststring);

        return 0;
}
```

Printing the string will result to this:

Figure 25: String Array

If you need to accept string user input, assign the value to a character array. Here's a sample code that you can use as a template:

```
#include<stdio.h>

int main()
{
            char name_array[10];
            char *ptr_name;

            printf("Enter your name and
press enter\n");
            scanf("%s", name_array);
            ptr_name = name_array;
            printf("Hi %s! \n",
ptr_name);

            return 0;
}
```

Input

Jenny

Output

Enter your name and press enter
Hi Jenny!

Figure 26: User Input Array

String Functions

C offers different string functions accessed via the string.h or strings.h library. Don't forget to include this in the code after the <stdio.h> declaration.

I will discuss some of the most commonly used functions when working with strings:

strcpy

This is used to copy the contents of one string to another.

Syntax:

```
strcpy (string1, string2);
```

String2 will be copied to string1.

strcat

Appends or concatenates the strings.

Syntax:

```
strcat (string1, string2);
```

strlen

Outputs the length of the given string.

Syntax:

```
strlen (string1);
```

Here's a sample code showcasing some of the functions discussed above:

```c
#include <stdio.h>
#include <string.h>
int main () {
    char str1[12] = "Hello ";
    char str2[12] = "there!";
    char str3[12];
    int len ;

    strcpy(str3, str1);
    printf("strcpy( str3, str1) :  %s\n", str3 );

    strcat( str1, str2);
    printf("strcat( str1, str2):  %s\n", str1 );

    len = strlen(str1);
    printf("strlen(str1) :  %d\n", len );

    return 0;
}
```

Output

```
strcpy( str3, str1) :  Hello
strcat( str1, str2):  Hello there!
strlen(str1) :  12
```

Figure 27: String Functions Output

79

In this chapter, you've learned how to give your programs more structure by using pointers, arrays, and strings. In the next chapter, you will learn about Command Line Arguments. After that, we'll put together all the things that you have learned and create your program!

Chapter Seven: Command Line Arguments

This chapter will discuss Command Line Arguments.

In C programming, it is perfectly possible to accept and to have command line arguments. These arguments are typically provided after the program name in the operating systems of the command line. Some of these operating systems include Linux and DOS. Command line arguments are then passed on to the created program from your operating system.

To utilize these command line arguments in the created program, you need to completely understand the entire declaration for the main function first. This main function should previously have no arguments to begin with.

Interestingly, the main function can simultaneously accept two types of arguments. The first one would be the number of the command line arguments. The second one would be the entire list of every command line argument included in the program.

The main argument's full declaration somehow appears like this:

```
int main ( int argc, char *argv[] )
```

For this code, argc is considered as the **argument count**. The argument count is the given number of command line arguments passed on to the created program. The command line is the origin for this argument. The line argument includes the program's name as well.

The array of the pointers for the character is regarded as the listing of every argument. On the other hand, argv[0] will be the program's name. For the declaration above, it is an empty string in case the name is not yet available. After this, every number of the element in the declaration that is less than the argc string will be considered as one of the command line arguments.

You may handle the command line arguments using main() as your function argument. If you combine it with other commands, argc will be considered as the number of passed arguments. On the other hand, argv[] will be the pointed array. This means that argv[] will point the each of the passed argument to the created program.

You may use each of the argv elements in the same way that you will use a string. Also, you may utilize argv and treat it as a type of two- dimensional kind of array. In any case, the argv[argc] will be considered a null pointer.

The following is an example that can help you check if there are any supplied arguments from the program's command line. Based on what you observed, you can take the necessary action.

```c
#include <stdio.h>

int main( int argc, char *argv[] ) {

    if( argc == 2 ) {
            printf("The supplied argument is %s\n", argv[1]);
    }
    else if( argc > 2 ) {
            printf("Too many supplied arguments.\n");
    }
    else {
            printf("Only one expected argument.\n");

    }

}
```

Compiling and executing the code above without passing any type of argument will eventually yield this result:

$./a.out

One expected argument

If you compile the codes above, and execute them using just one argument, it can produce this result:

$./a/out testing

The supplied argument is testing.

On the other hand, if you compile the codes above and execute them using two arguments, it can produce this result:

$./a/out testing1 testing2

Too many supplied arguments.

Take note that the argv[0] is considered the bearer of the program name itself. On the other hand, argv[1] serves as the pointer to your first supplied command line. Given these facts, *argv[n] will be regarded as the last argument. If you do not supply any argument, argc will be considered as one of those. Otherwise, passing one argument will then set argc to 2.

You have to pass all of the command line arguments, and separate them using spaces. However, if the argument itself contains a space, you need to pass this argument by placing them inside quotation marks. You may also use single quotes, or '' for this. To illustrate this, here is an example:

```c
#include <stdio.h>

int main( int argc, char *argv[] ) {

    printf("Program's name %s\n", argv[0]);

    if( argc == 2 ) {
            printf("The supplied argument is %s\n", argv[1]);
    }
    else if( argc > 2 ) {
            printf("Too many supplied arguments.\n");
    }
    else {
            printf("One expected argument.\n");
    }
}
```

If you try compiling and executing the code above using a single argument with spaces enclosed within single quotation marks or double quotation marks, it can produce this result:

$./a.out "testing1 testing2"

Program's name ./a.out
The supplied argument is testing1 testing2

It is actually easy to use this argument for your program. Almost any type of program that prefers the parameters set as soon as the program is executed, will definitely use this one. One of the most common uses for this is to create a function that can take the name of a specific given file. The output would be the entire text of the file. This will be displayed on the screen.

```
#include <stdic.h>

int main ( int argc, char *argv[] )
{
   if ( argc != 1) /* argc should be 1 for right execution */
   {
           /* I print argv[0] assuming this is the program's
name */
           Printf( "usage: %s filename", argv[0] );
   }
   else
   }
           // I assume argv[1] will be the filename to be
opened
           FILE *file = fopen( argv[1], "r" );

           /* fopen returns 0, the NULL pointer, during
failure */
           if ( file == 0 )
           {
                   printf ( "unable to open file\n" );
           }
           else
           {
                   int x;
                   /* from the file, read one character only at a
                   time, stop at FOF, which somewhat
```
86

indicates the file's ending. Take note
that the idiom stating that "assign it to
one variable, then check the value"
used at the bottom part will work
because the statement of the assignment
eventually evaluates to the assigned
value. */

```c
while ( ( x = fgetc ( file ) ) != EOF )
{
        printf ( "%c", x );
}
fclose ( file );
            }
        }
    }
}
```

The program above is relatively short. However, it has
effectively incorporated the full version of the main declaration. It
even performed one useful function. First, it checks to fully
ensure that the program user successfully included the second
argument. Theoretically, this will be the file name. The program
will then perform another check to verify if the file is valid. This
is done by opening the file in question. This is considered a
standard operation type. If the operation eventually leads to the
opening of the file, then fopen's return value will have a valid
FILE*; as the output. In case the opposite is true, that will be 0. In
this case, 0 is considered as the NULL pointer.

After this, you just have to execute a loop. The loop will be
used to help you print out one character, for instance. The code is
somewhat self-explanatory. However, it has some comments

included in it. You will have little trouble deciphering how the operation works if you look at it carefully.

Typecasting

Typecasting is considered a way to change one variable from one type of date to another, different kind of data. It is a method of making one variable into one type, like the int variable, to another different type of variable, like the char. This is done for a single operation. For instance, if you are thinking of storing one 'long' value to a kind of simple integer, all you have to do is to type cast the string 'long' into 'int'.

You may even convert your values from one kind to another by explicitly utilizing the cast operator.

(type_name) expression

This example will show you that the cast operator can cause division of an integer variable by another one. It will be performed as a kind of floating point operation.

```
#include <stdio.h>

main*( {

    int sum = 20, count = 4;
    double mean;

    mean = (double) sum / count;
    printf("Value of mean : %f\n", mean );

}
```

If you compile and execute the code given above, it will produce this result:

Value of mean : 5.00000

Take note that your cast operator should have precedence over the division. Therefore, the value of **sum** command should first be converted to type **double**. Finally, it should be divided by count. This will eventually yield a double value.

Some type conversions may be implicit. You may automatically perform this function yourself if you prefer. An alternative would be to explicitly specify this by using the cast operator. Using your cast operator when type conversions are needed is actually considered a good practice, as far as programming is concerned.

If you want to typecast a program or an operation, you have to place the variable type, that you prefer the actual variable to, act within the inside parentheses. These should be placed directly in front of your actual preferred variable. For instance, (char)a will create the 'a' function as char.

Here is an example of typecasting "in action":

```
#include <stdio.h>

int main()
{
/* The (char) is considered a typecast. This instructs the
    computer to interpret the number 65 as a type of
    character and not merely as a number. This will
    provide the character with an output for the equivalent
    for the number 65 (In the case of ASCII, this will be
    the letter A). Take note that the %c found below will
    be considered as the format code of printing just one
    character.
*/
printf( "%c\n". (char) 65 );
getchar ();
}
```

One of the main uses of typecasting is highlighted if you prefer to use some ASCII characters. For instance, in case you want to come up with your own chart of all the 128 ASCII characters, you need to use the typecast function. This will permit you to print out all the integers as the character equivalent.

```c
#include <stdio.h>

int main()
{
    for ( int x = 0; x < 128; x++ ) {
        /* Note the function of int type for x to provide output and use
         * of (char) tohelp typecast x to a character that outputs
         * ASCII characters that correspond to current number
         */
        printf( "%d = %c\n", x, (char)x );
    }
    getchar();

}
```

If you look closely, you will notice something really strange. If you pass the x value to printf to pass off as a char, in theory, it is expected that the intended value will be treated as a type of character when you write the format string as %c. Because the char variety is considered a relatively small integer, adding the typecast will not actually add any form of value to it!

Therefore, the typecast will come in handy if you want to force the right kind of mathematical operation, and have it take place in the program successfully. It will eventually turn out that in C and other types of programming languages, the final output of the integer divisions is also itself treated as another integer. For example, a value of ¼ turns to 0 because this is considered less than a whole number. The process of dividing integers eventually ignores the remaining value.

On the other hand, the division between the floating- point numbers and even between the floating- point number and the integer is enough to make the result show up as a type of floating point number. Therefore, if you are planning to execute a type of fancy division that you do not want to have truncated values, you will need to cast one of your variables into a floating- point kind. For example, (float)¼ will come out as a .25, as per normal expectation.

It is usually reasonable for you to store two different values in the integers. If you are tracking patients with heart problems, you can have a specific function that will help you compute for the age of each patient in years. You may also include the specific number of instances that they came in for complaints, like heart pain. One type of operation that you may want to execute is the frequency of visits that a patient had with their physician, because of angina or heart pain. For this particular situation, the program will look something like this:

```
/* function will return age in years */
int age = getAge();
```

```
/* function will return number of visits */
int angina_visits = getVisits();

float visits_per_year = angina_visits / age;
```

The only problem is when you run the created program, the visits_per_year string will give an output of zero. This will take place unless the patient with the heart problem had a really large number of clinic visits for the duration of the entire year. One way to help you resolve this problem is by casting one of the given values that will be divided. This will then be treated as a kind of floating point number. In turn, it will cause you to treat this expression like it were really bound to be a floating- point number:

```
float visits_per_year = angina_visits / (float)age;
/* or */
float visits_per_year = (float)angina_visits / age;
```

Using this sequence will eventually bring in the right values. These values will be stored in the visits_per_year string. Aside from the example shown above, you may even come up with other similar programs to resolve the problem.

Integer Promotion

Integer promotion is the method of converting values with integer types that are smaller than unsigned int or int to unsigned int or int. See the example below:

```
#include <stdio.h>

main() {

    int i = 1;
    char c = 'c'; /* ascii value is 9 */
    int sum;

    sum = i + c;
    printf("Value of sum : %d\n", sum );

}
```

If you compile and execute the code above, it will produce this result:

Value of sum: 10

For this particular example, the value of the sum is 10 because you resorted to integer promotion. You also converted the 'c' value to ASCII before you performed the actually operation of addition.

In this chapter, we discussed command line arguments. In the next chapter, get ready to create your first program!

Great progress so far!

Chapter Eight: Creating Your First Program

In this chapter, you will create your first program, exciting times!

Now that you have learned what you can use in your program, it's time to take all the skills that you learned in this book and combine them into a single program. It doesn't have to be so hard. You can try just coding something to let everyone know your program is up and running!

Here's a sample program that you can do.

Suppose a user wants to generate prime numbers. You need to come up with a program that will give the first X prime numbers depending on how many prime numbers the user wants to generate.

First, we need to understand what prime numbers are. Prime numbers are integers whose only divisor is one and itself. Between numbers 1 to 10, there are four prime numbers. These are 2, 3, 5, and 7. When the user says he wants 4 prime numbers, your program should generate 2, 3, 5, and 7.

There are many ways on how you can create a program for this one. Here's one way that you can do:

```c
#include<stdio.h>

int main()
{
    int n, i = 3, count, c;
```

```c
        printf("How many prime numbers do you want to
generate?\n");
        scanf("%d",&n);

        if ( n >= 1 )
        {
            printf("Here are the first %d prime
numbers :\n",n);
            printf("2\n");
        }

        for ( count = 2 ; count <= n ;  )
        {
            for ( c = 2 ; c <= i - 1 ; c++ )
            {
                if ( i%c == 0 )
                    break;
            }
            if ( c == i )
            {
                printf("%d\n",i);
                count++;
            }
            i++;
        }

        return 0;
    }
```

Now, try the program and see how it will generate prime
numbers.

Input

```
4
```

Output

```
How many prime numbers do you want to generate?
Here are the first 4 prime numbers :
2
3
5
7
```

Figure 28: Output for Prime Numbers

Another way that you can do is to create a function and call the function within the program. With what you've learned in the previous chapters, I'm confident that you can convert that program into one with a prime number function checker.

This is the end of the teaching chapters for beginners in C programming. In the next chapter, I'll be providing more sample exercises that you can use to practice your newly acquired programming skills.

Chapter Nine: Exercises

In this final chapter, I have laid out a number of exercises that you can try out, to test what you've learned. If, in case, you feel like you cannot initially figure out the logic behind the program, take the time to analyze and try again. Get a pen and paper too! It helps to put logic down in writing.

All the best!

Exercise #1:

Write a program that will take any given number and display it in the reverse order.

Answer #1:

```c
#include <stdio.h>

int main()
{
    int n, numreverse = 0;

    printf("Give me a number and I'll show
it in reverse:\n");
    scanf("%d", &n);

    while (n != 0)
    {
        numreverse = numreverse * 10;
        numreverse = numreverse + n%10;
        n        = n/10;
    }

    printf("The number when reversed is
%d\n", reverse);

    return 0;
}
```

Here's a sample output:

Input

```
123456789
```

Output

```
Give me a number and I'll show it in reverse:
The number when reversed is 987654321
```

Figure 29: Output of Numreverse

Exercise #2:

Create a program that will get user input of two strings and then concatenate these strings. Hint: use the built-in *strcat* function in C.

Answer #2:

```c
#include <stdio.h>
#include <string.h>

int main()
{
    char word1[1000], word2[1000];

    printf("What's the first word?\n");
    scanf("%s", &word1);

    printf("And the second word?\n");
    scanf("%s", &word2);

    strcat(word1,word2);

    printf("Put these two words together
and you'll get %s\n",word1);

    return 0;
}
```

Now, put in strings and see if the code will work:

Input

```
butter
fly
```

Output

```
What's the first word?
And the second word?
Put these two words together and you'll get butterfly
```

Figure 30: Concatenate Strings Output

Exercise #3:

Supposed you were asked to process data input to convert all inputs to upper case letters. How would you create a program for this? *Hint:* use the *toupper* function in C.

Answer #3:

```c
#include <stdio.h>
#include <ctype.h>

int main()
{
    int counter = 0;
    char word1[1000];
    printf("What word do you want to
convert to upper string?\n");
    scanf("%s", &word1);

    while(word1[counter])
    {
        putchar (toupper(word1[counter]));
        counter++;
    }

    return(0);
}
```

Enter a word in varied letter cases and see how the program will process the input word.

Input

```
ThiS
```

Output

```
What word do you want to convert to upper string?
THIS
```

That's it. Well done!

Turn to the next page to see a quick recap of what you have learned in this course. Don't forget to stay until the end to claim your free video course training!

Recap

Here is a quick recap of what we covered, in case you need a refresher on a certain step:

1. You now have an understanding of what the C Programming language is -- its features, benefits and its capabilities.
2. You have learned about operators, pointers, arrays, and strings.
3. You now know how to structure codes, understand variables, if statements, loops, switch cases, as well as other functions.
4. You have created a program (aside from the Hello World program, of course!)
5. You have practiced creating programs for complex exercises.

Turn to the next page to gain access to a free video course, and to also see my other best-selling books, which are part of this series!

Before You Go

Congratulations! You have reached the end of this step-by-step course and have learned a lot on the way.

I've done my best to gather all my knowledge to share with you what I've learned about C programming.

Your next step is to implement what you've learned. Become a master of C programming language and create your own programs. What's good about C language is that learning all about it will make it easy for you to branch out on other, more advanced programming languages, which is something I strongly recommend if you want to really develop your abilities.

The great news is that because you have gone through this course, you will be astonished to find that your learning other languages is easier than expected. C has strikingly paved the way for you. You can find other popular programming books by visiting our full library at >> http://amzn.to/1Xxmab2

I would also really appreciate your reviews and your feedback. If you really enjoyed this book, then feel free to share it so other people may also profit from this information.

Finally, you can also send me an email if you have any questions, feedback or just want to say hello! (I do reply!) My email address is; (Felix_Alvaro@mail.com)

I thank you once again and God bless!

Before We Continue, Here Are Other Books Our Readers Loved!

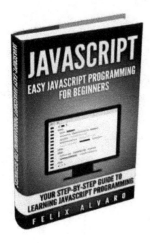

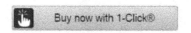

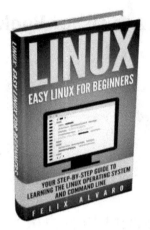

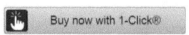

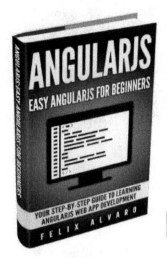

Learn AngularJS
Web-App Developing
Today With This Easy,
Step-By-Step Guide

★★★★★

Buy now with 1-Click®

http://amzn.to/1pDg0BZ

Learn Python Programming
Today With This Easy,
Step-By-Step Guide!

★★★★★

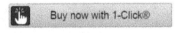

Buy now with 1-Click®

http://amzn.to/1WOBiy2

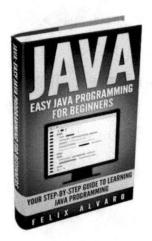

Learn Java Programming
Today With This Easy,
Step-By-Step Guide!

Buy now with 1-Click®

http://amzn.to/1WTgUw0

#1 Best Seller in Functional Analysis

All You Need To Learn
To Drive Tons Of Traffic
To Your Website Today!

Buy now with 1-Click®

http://amzn.to/21HWFWb

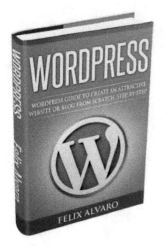

Easily Create Your Own
Eye-Catching, Professional
Website or Blog Using
WordPress Today!

http://amzn.to/1VHtxZi

www.ingramcontent.com/pod-product-compliance
Lightning Source LLC
Chambersburg PA
CBHW071227050326
40689CB00011B/2484